Pizza Parts

by Kathy Furgang

T5-AFP-809

Table of Contents

How Do Cooks Use Math in the Kitchen?

Have you ever tasted food made with too much pepper or too many onions? Yuck! A cook's job is to make food taste good by combining just the right amounts of foods together. To do that, a little math is needed.

Every food that is used to cook something is called an **ingredient**. Each ingredient adds flavor to a food. Each ingredient is a **fraction**, or part, that makes up the whole food.

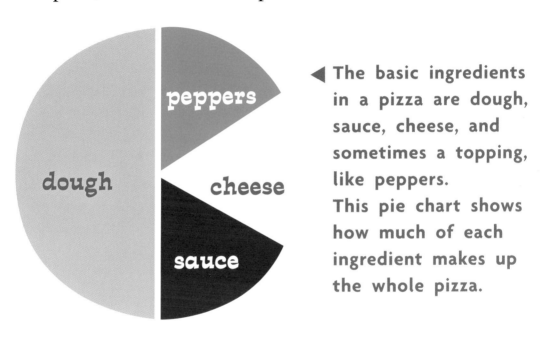

◀ The basic ingredients in a pizza are dough, sauce, cheese, and sometimes a topping, like peppers.
This pie chart shows how much of each ingredient makes up the whole pizza.

▼ This chart shows the same parts in another way.

How Do You Read Fractions?

This pizza is cut into eight equal slices.
Each slice of pizza is one equal part of the who
What fraction of the pizza is one slice? It is on
slice out of eight, or ¹/₈ of the pie.

What fraction of ▶
the pie is 3 slices?
It's ³/₈ of the pie.

$$\frac{3}{8}$$

Pizza Problems

Draw a pizza and divide it into four equal
slices. Color ³/₄ of the pie. How much of the
pie is not colored?

The shape of the whole does not affect the fractions. A square pizza can be cut into eight slices also. Each part is equal in size to the others. And each part is one out of eight, or ⅛ of the whole pizza.

▲ What fraction of the pizza is 7 slices? The whole pizza is 8 slices. So it's ⅞ of the pizza.

The number on the bottom of a fraction is called the **denominator**. It tells how many parts make up the whole. The **numerator** is the number on top. It tells how many parts of the whole you are talking about.

The numerator tells how many parts of the whole you are talking about.
▼

$$\frac{2}{5}$$

▲
The denominator tells how many parts are in the whole.

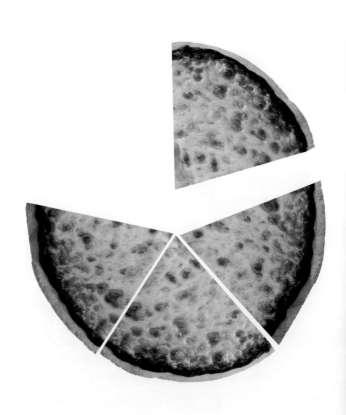

The bigger the number in the denominator, the smaller each part of the whole will be.

The smaller the number in the denominator, the bigger each part of the whole will be.

Which is a bigger fraction, $\frac{1}{5}$ or $\frac{1}{3}$?

Pizza Problems

The photo on page 6 shows the fraction $\frac{2}{5}$. How would the picture have to change in order to show $\frac{3}{5}$?

How Do You Make a Pizza?

Pizzas can be made out of just about any ingredients you can think of. Most pizzas are made with dough, tomato sauce, and mozzarella cheese. But you can experiment with different sauces, cheeses, and toppings on your pizza.

You can put almost any food on a pizza. This pizza has hot peppers, chicken, tomatoes, and olives. ▶

Pizza Stories

The earliest pizzas were flat, crispy breads eaten by the early Greeks thousands of years ago. They topped the breads with olive oils and spices.

To make a pizza that tastes good, you need to use fractions. Too much or too little of an ingredient can make your pizza taste funny. Imagine a pizza made of $^7/_{10}$ sauce and $^3/_{10}$ dough. Would that taste good?

People use special cups and spoons for measuring pizza ingredients. The same measurement can be made every time. The pictures show the measuring tools you will need to make a pizza.

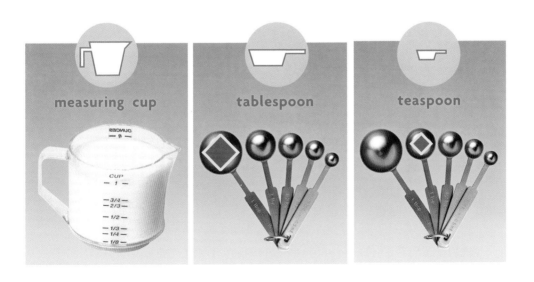

measuring cup   tablespoon   teaspoon

How Do You Make the Pizza Dough?

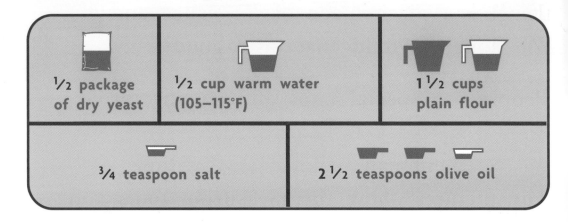

½ package of dry yeast

½ cup warm water (105–115°F)

1½ cups plain flour

¾ teaspoon salt

2½ teaspoons olive oil

An adult can help you get the water to the right temperature at the sink. Stir the yeast and warm water together in a bowl. Let the yeast mixture stand for a few minutes until you see bubbles form. The yeast is not working if you do not see bubbles.

Add the flour, salt, and 1½ teaspoons of the olive oil. Stir until the dough forms and makes a ball in the center of the bowl.

Flour is an important ingredient in dough. Just the right fraction of flour is needed to make the dough. If you add too much flour, the dough will be dry and stiff and difficult to **knead**. Kneading is pressing the dough with your hands. If you don't add enough flour, the dough will stick to the bowl and your fingers, and it will not come together properly.

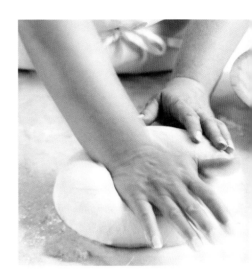

Pizza Problems

This recipe will make enough dough for one 12-inch pizza. What would you do if you wanted to make two 12-inch pizzas? Use the pictures of the ingredients to double the recipe.

1. Sprinkle flour on a flat work surface before putting down your dough.

2. Push down into the ball of dough with your hands.

An adult can help you knead the mixture. Knead for about three to five minutes to form a smooth ball. Place one teaspoon of oil into the bowl. Roll the ball of dough in the oil. Cover the bowl with plastic wrap.

Pizza Stories

The earliest pizzas were flat because they were not made with yeast. Italian Queen Margherita traveled around the countryside of Italy in the 1880s. She saw people eating flat bread. She tried the pizza for the first time and it quickly became one of her favorite foods.

3. Use one hand to lift the dough and push it back into itself. Repeat with each hand again and again.

4. Sprinkle some extra flour on the dough if it starts to get sticky.

Yeast makes dough rise. The dough will double in size. It will take about 45 minutes for the dough to finish rising. That's ¾ of an hour.

The shaded part of the clock shows ¾ of an hour.

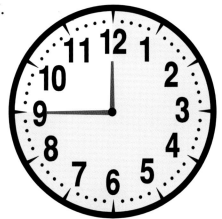

How Do You Make the Sauce?

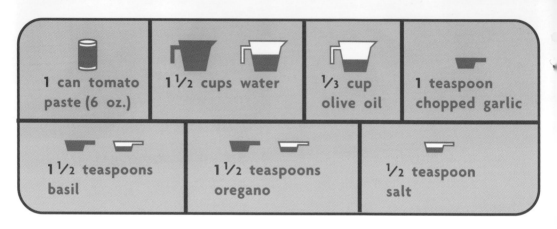

1 can tomato paste (6 oz.)	1½ cups water	⅓ cup olive oil	1 teaspoon chopped garlic
1½ teaspoons basil	1½ teaspoons oregano	½ teaspoon salt	

Ask an adult to work with you when you cut up ingredients or use the stove.

Mix the tomato paste, water, and olive oil in a pan. Heat the mixture and stir it. Add the garlic, basil, oregano, and salt. Set the sauce aside until it's time to put it on the dough.

It's not time to cook your pizza yet, but it is time to turn on the oven. Have an adult set the oven to 475 degrees. It takes about 1/4 of an hour, or 15 minutes, for the oven to reach the right temperature. This is called preheating.

▲ Food cooks best in an oven that has reached the right temperature.

◄ You can also use sauce from a jar on your pizza. But this recipe gives you good practice using fractions!

Pizza Stories

The first modern pizza was invented in 1889 by a chef in Naples. He was asked to make a special meal for a visit from pizza-lover Queen Margherita. He made her a pizza topped with tomatoes, cheese, and basil. He chose these foods for their colors: red, white, and green—the colors of the Italian flag.

What Goes on the Pizza?

After the dough rises, press it into a 12-inch circle on a baking sheet. You can do this by flattening it out with your hands and your fingers. Next, spoon the sauce onto the pizza dough to cover it.

◀ Don't cover the edges of the dough with sauce. The plain edge is the crust that allows you to pick up the pizza without getting your fingers messy.

Now it's time for the pizza toppings. Cheese is the most popular topping. Sprinkle shredded cheese on top of the sauce. **Estimate**, or guess, what fraction of the package of cheese you used. Was it $1/2$? Was it $3/4$?

You can put other toppings on top of the pizza, too. If you like meat, green peppers, and cheese on your pizza, you could make $1/3$ of your toppings meat, $1/3$ green peppers, and $1/3$ cheese.

What if you are sharing a pizza, but you and your friend don't like the same toppings? You might put pepperoni on $1/2$ of your pizza and mushrooms on the other $1/2$ of your pizza.

How Many Slices Can You Make?

Now the oven should be hot enough to cook your pizza. Have an adult place the pizza in the oven. Bake it for 10 to 15 minutes. The crust will become golden brown and the cheese will melt and begin to bubble.

Now the pizza is ready to cut and eat!

These pictures show pizzas sliced into different fractions. How many pizza fractions can you make?

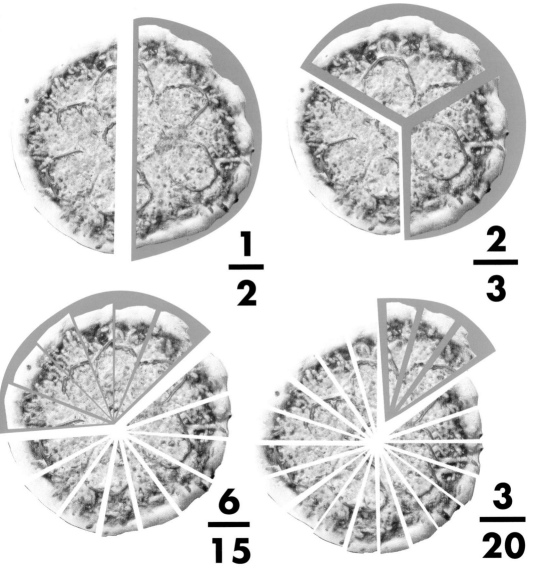

$$\frac{1}{2}$$

$$\frac{2}{3}$$

$$\frac{6}{15}$$

$$\frac{3}{20}$$

Glossary

denominator (dih-NAH-mih-nay-ter): the number of parts a whole is divided into; the bottom number in a fraction

estimate (ES-tih-mate): to guess

fraction (FRAK-shun): part of a whole

ingredient (in-GREE-dee-ent): every food that is used to cook something; part of a whole recipe

knead (NEED): to press with your hands

numerator (NOO-muh-ray-ter): the number of parts you are talking about; the upper number in a fraction

---

Index